Celebrating
Wiltshire

Heather Robinson

Other works by Heather Robinson, all available to purchase via Amazon:

Wall of Stone – full length fiction set in Roman Britain

Our Book: The Sharing Book - a collection of short stories for adults, and puzzle stories for children

Stour Valley Way in Pictures – a collection of photographs taken along this Long Distance Footpath

Outline Map of Wiltshire
Inset Map: Position of Wiltshire in England

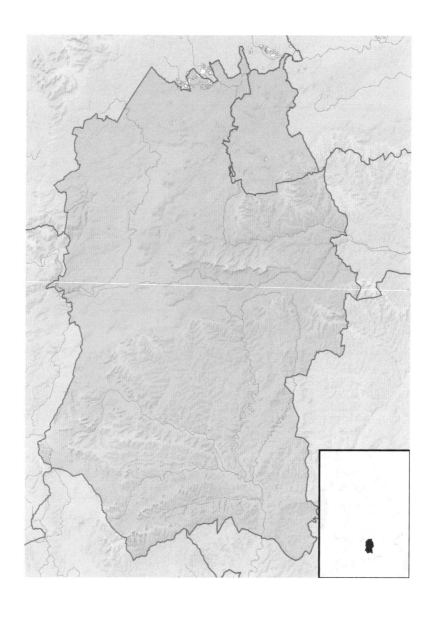

Map of Wiltshire with Towns

Introduction

Almost half of the Wiltshire landscape falls within an Area of Outstanding Natural Beauty. Ancient by-ways, trails and paths, around 8200 of them, steeped in legend and fuelled by folklore, lace the countryside together. Wiltshire offers peaceful, glorious countryside and will show you rural England at its very best.

You will know of the UNESCO World Heritage Site of Avebury and Stonehenge and doubtless heard of the iconic white horses carved into the rolling chalk downs and the awe-inspiring Salisbury Cathedral with one of the finest original copies of Magna Carta and the tallest spire in Britain. Longleat Safari Park, Old Sarum, Stourhead, Lacock, Bowood House and Old Wardour Castle are all renowned tourist attractions and worthy of your attention.

As if that isn't enough, I would like to give you further reasons to visit this charming county and to celebrate its quirks and beauty.

Ten sets of clues will lead you to ten places you may not know: towns, monuments and features. All can be reached by car, cycle, on foot and most by public transport.

Solve the clues, learn the history and explore Wiltshire, a county for all seasons!

You will find confirmation of the destinations at the back of the book, plus some helpful websites for the tourist attractions mentioned above.

Gravestone of Hannah Twynnoy mentioned in Destination One

Destination One

- I am the oldest borough of England and the capital town of the first King of England.

- Eilmer, an 11th Century monk flew from the tower of my abbey, soaring 200 yards before falling to break both his legs. Look for his stained glass window in my abbey.

- I contain a 500 year old Market Cross.

- Charles I is said to have hidden here during the English Civil War.

- Two rivers form a natural moat around me.

- In 1703, a maid by the name of Hannah Twynnoy was mauled to death here by a tiger from a travelling circus. Her gravestone poem can still be seen in my abbey grounds:

> "In bloom of life,
> She's snatched from hence,
> She had not room to make defence,
> For tyger fierce,
> Took life away,
> And here she lies,
> In a bed of clay,
> Until the resurrection day."

- I am on the southern edge of the Cotswolds.

Destination Two on a frosty day

Destination Two

- I am a red brick folly with a stone top and stand 160 feet (46 metres) high.

- My triangular shape straddles the Wiltshire/Somerset border.

- I mark the start of the 28 mile Leland Trail – a footpath that leads to Ham Hill Country Park in South Somerset.

- Egbert's stone, where it is believed troops were rallied in 878 for the Battle of Ethandun is located nearby.

- Henry Hoare II commissioned me to commemorate the end of the Seven Years War and the accession of George III to the throne in 1760.

- I lie at the north western edge of a National Trust estate.

Both photos on this page can be found at
Destination Three

Destination Three

- I am a ghost village, six miles from any town.

- You need to check I am open before visiting me, as access is restricted by the military.

- I have no postcode.

- There is believed to have been a settlement here since 967. The Doomsday Book, completed in 1086, records there being seven households.

- Villagers were given forty-seven days to leave their homes in 1943 to allow US troops to prepare for D-Day landings. They were never allowed to return.

- The Churches Conservation Trust now cares for my church, St Giles Church, which stands proudly on higher ground and the remains of medieval paintings can be seen on the walls, including a set of 17th Century bell ringing changes.

- I have a twin ghost village in Dorset called Tyneham.

Frosty countryside on the outskirts of Destination Four

Destination Four

- I am a garrison town in West Wiltshire, with my origins lying in the corn trade.

- The 1960's brought me fame as a 'UFO' hotspot.

- A chapel that is owned by the townspeople and exists outside the control of the Church of England sits in my High Street. It is held in trust by twelve feoffees who are responsible for its preservation and upkeep. The chapel takes its name from the saint who was martyred by the Romans by being roasted to death on a gridiron. His festival date is 10th August.

- Opposite this chapel is a Victorian theatre designed by W.J. Stent.

- Within a short distance of my centre, I have a splendid boating lake and park.

- Lions roam the land just four miles from me.

The Moot in Destination Five

Destination Five

- I am an attractive 14th Century borough of thatched cottages and village greens.

- Surrounded by water meadows and chalk downlands, I bestride the River Avon.

- My Moot, now ornamental gardens, is a reputed Saxon meeting place and parliament.

- Robert 'Bonnie Bobby' Shafto, the most likely subject of the famous nursery rhyme was a Member of Parliament for me.

> *Bobby Shafto's gone to sea,*
> *Silver buckles on his knee;*
> *He'll come back and marry me,*
> *Bonnie Bobby Shafto!*
> *Bobby Shafto's bright and fair,*
> *Combing down his yellow hair;*
> *He's my love for evermair,*
> *Bonnie Bobby Shafto!*

- The Cuckoo Fair, a feature of village life since the 16th Century with maypole and Morris dancing, rural crafts and fare, is still held here annually on the first Bank Holiday Saturday of May.

- I am situated just outside the New Forest National Park.

The Gold Post Box in Destination Six

Destination Six

- My origins are Roman and I lie partly in the Avon Valley.

- I host a gold post box in honour of Ed McKeever's canoeing gold medal at the 2012 Summer Olympics held in London.

- Shaftesbury Abbey, the richest nunnery in Medieval England, once owned my tithe barn which is one of the finest 14th Century barns to be built, with an amazing timber cruck roof.

- I have an old, but widened packhorse bridge with a town lock-up sporting a weather vane in the form of a gudgeon; the colloquial name given to a person born and bred in this town.

- You will find a small Saxon church in my midst.

- A two mile walk from me will take you to the impressive aqueduct that carries the Kennet and Avon Canal over the River Avon.

The One-sided Roman Bridge

Village Houses made from Cotswold Stone

Destination Seven

- Often referred to as the prettiest village in Britain, I lie where the Cotswolds meet the Wiltshire Downs.

- The ancient Fosse Way passes close by.

- The village houses are all constructed in Cotswold stone with thick walls and roofs made from split natural stone tiles. The properties are many hundreds of years old and are listed as ancient monuments.

- At the far end of the village is a one-sided bridge, often referred to as the 'Roman Bridge' and one local story says that the ghost of a Roman Centurion still guards this crossing.

- I was a weaving community in the Middle Ages and possibly the 'home of the blanket' as a second local story claims that two brothers by the name of Blanket, finding their weavers' cottage somewhat chilly, wove a heavy, raised nap cloth that they wrapped around themselves at night for warmth. Others followed suit, naming their new bed cloth after the brothers.

- The fastest sporting location in the south west of England lies half a mile from me.

A Turnstile found in the area below the National Nature Reserve in Destination Eight

Destination Eight

- I am a National Nature Reserve on a steep south-facing scarp slope with superb panoramic views over the vale below.

- My area is known for crop circles in summer.

- The highest point of Wiltshire at 965 feet (294.19 metres) is nearby.

- I am in the area of an Anglo-Saxon battle site, where the ancient passages of Wansdyke and the Ridgeway interconnect.

- My surrounding topography is undulated by neolithic long barrows of which Adam's Grave is an impressive example.

- The pub of a nearby village was host to Carlton Television's production of Colin Dexter's "The Wench is Dead", an Inspector Morse whodunit.

The Leipzig Plantation

The Reflective Pool

Destination Nine

- I am a park with a reflective pool, a Quaker burial site, a small aviary and an array of play equipment.

- You will find me in the same town which is famous for the legend of the Moonrakers – Wiltshire's smuggling story.

- Less than two miles to my north is the Victorian Leipzig Plantation, believed to be named after the crucial battle of the Napoleonic Wars in 1813, with its stunning avenue of beautiful beech trees that overlooks my town.

- An iron age earthwork fortress, Oliver's Castle, is also in this area, and given its name sometime after the 13th July 1643, the date of a key battle in the English Civil War where the Royalists defeated Oliver Cromwell's Parliamentarians on this hill.

- Within two miles to my south, you will find the unusual scheduled monument of a steep flight of sixteen locks. This flight of locks was engineer John Rennie's solution to climbing the very steep hill, and was the last part of the 87 mile route of the Kennet and Avon canal to be completed.

- A Victorian Brewery can be visited less than a mile from me.

A Squirrel and Named Tree Sign in Destination Ten

Destination Ten

- Big Belly, the oldest oak tree in the country with a bulging 35 foot girth (10.76 metres), can be found on my perimeter. Experts say that this Big Belly Oak – named as one of the fifty Great British Trees – has been growing since Alfred the Great was fighting the Vikings over one thousand years ago.

- King Henry VIII's third wife, Jane Seymour – mother of King Edward VI – was the daughter of my warden Sir John Seymour in the mid-1500's.

- I extend to an area of 4500 acres and am the only privately owned forest in Britain.

- Britain's longest tree-lined avenue sits at my heart. It is just under four miles long and was created by "England's Greatest Gardener", Lancelot Capability Brown.

- The English rock band Radiohead named their album King of Limbs after another of my ancient trees.

- In 1789 the 110 foot (33.85 metres) Ailesbury Column was erected on the brow of one of my hills, partly to commemorate King George III's recovery from madness, although the column remained intact much longer than the monarch's health, as his affliction returned to stay a couple of years later.

Facts and Figures

OS Maps covering Wiltshire:
Explorer Map 130,141,142,143,156,157,169

Wiltshire covers an area of 1344 square miles.

Two thirds of the county is built on chalk.

The county measures 55 miles north to south, and 34 miles east to west.

The highest point in Wiltshire is 965 feet (294.19 metres).

Wiltshire has nearly 4000 miles of Rights
of Way, including:
The Ridgeway - National Trail
The Mid-Wilts Way - Long Distance Footpath
The White Horse Way - Long Distance Footpath
The Monarch's Way - Long Distance Footpath
The Wessex Ridgeway - Long Distance Footpath
The Imber Range Perimeter Path - Long Distance Footpath

There are 30 rivers in total in Wiltshire.

List of Visible White Horses in Wiltshire

Name	Date	OS Grid Reference
Westbury	1778	ST898516
Cherhill	1780	SU049696
Marlborough	1804	SU184682
Alton Barnes	1812	SU106637
Hackpen	1838	SU128749
Broad Town	1864	SU098783
Pewsey	1937	SU171580
Devizes	1999	SU016641

Wiltshire is *the* county for white horses, with thirteen of the known twenty-four hill figures in Britain having been carved into the chalk downs of central Wiltshire.

Of the thirteen white horses known to have existed in Wiltshire, eight are still visible, the other five having been reclaimed by the turf.

The newest of the white horses, the Devizes Horse, is the only one in Wiltshire to face to the right. It was designed by Peter Greed and cut by around two hundred local people in 1999 to commemorate the third millennium. It's position is about a mile from the old Devizes Horse, one of those to be lost to the turf. The old horse was known locally as the Snob's Horse as it was cut by the local shoemakers, and 'snob' is the Wiltshire dialect word for a shoemaker.

Answers to the Destinations

Destination One:
Malmesbury

Destination Two:
Alfred's Tower

Destination Three:
Imber Village

Destination Four:
Warminster

Destination Five:
Downton

Destination Six:
Bradford-on-Avon

Destination Seven:
Castle Combe

Destination Eight:
Pewsey Vale National Nature Reserve

Destination Nine:
Hillworth Park, Devizes SN10 5HB

Destination Ten:
Savernake Forest

Useful Websites

www.nationaltrust.org.uk/avebury

www.english-heritage.org.uk/visit/places/stonehenge

www.wiltshirewhitehorses.org.uk

www.salisburycathedral.org.uk

www.longleat.co.uk

www.english-heritage.org.uk/visit/places/old-sarum

www.nationaltrust.org.uk/stourhead

www.cotswolds.info/places/lacock.shtml

www.bowood.org

www.english-heritage.org.uk/visit/places/old-wardour-castle

www.canalrivertrust.org.uk/places-to-visit/52-caen-hill-locks

www.wiltshire.gov.uk/recreation-rights-of-way

www.wadworth.co.uk/more/brewery-tours/visiting-our-brewery

Grateful thanks to:
www.history.wiltshire.gov.uk/
www.visitwiltshire.co.uk

Printed in Great Britain
by Amazon

49240542R00017